The 1st Three Years of Acro,

Gymnastics, & Tumbling

Teaching Tips, Monthly Lesson Plans, and Syllabi for Successful Gymnastics Classes

By: Gina Evans

Frank, Noelle and Terry for the encouragement to write again.

The 1ˢᵗ Three Years of Acro, Gymnastics, & Tumbling

Teaching Tips, Monthly Lesson Plans, and Syllabi for Successful Gymnastics Classes

Introduction

After I wrote my first book, *The 1st Three Years of Dance: Teaching Tips, Monthly Lesson Plans, and Syllabi for Successful Dance* Classes, I realized what a need there was for such a book. Now, I have taken the same formula and applied my years of experience in gymnastics to write this book. There is no need to spend time continually developing classes each week, month, and year. With *The 1st Three Years of Acro, Gymnastics, & Tumbling: Teaching Tips, Monthly Lesson Plans, and Syllabi for Successful Gymnastics Classes,* you have a consistent base from which you and your teacher can teach.

Although so much of learning gymnastics is based on repetition, you need changes in the class from month to month and from level to level. This will show the untrained eyes of parents that gymnastics education is an ongoing process, and a student cannot learn it all in one year. This will also keep your classes from getting stale. In this book, the classes build on one another; by utilizing my progressive lesson plans, students will be given equal knowledge of the skills from one teacher to the next and from one class to the next.

This book also provides a perfect model for organizations besides gyms to learn how to add in a gymnastics program. As any savvy business owner knows, the best way to grow your business is to find new customers or to sell more to the customers you already have. Whether you are a dance studio, sport complex, or recreation center, *The 1st Three Years of Acro, Gymnastics, & Tumbling* gives you a step-by-step process for introducing a new program, which will allow you to benefit more from your pre-existing customers.

No matter if your program is completely new or you have been at it for 30 years, this book develops a common base from which all of your teachers can build their classes. Giving students a strong, balanced gymnastics education in their early years will allow students' individual talents, education, and creativity to thrive during classes in later years.

Chapter One
Teaching Tips

Safety First

The "safety first" principle applies to safety precautions you should take before, during, and after class. Do not let students enter the classroom area before class or allow them to play in the classroom afterward. Make sure all of your equipment is set up safely, correctly, and free of any potential obstacles. Also make sure you have the appropriate padding and mats out. Always do a walk-through safety check before each class, and remember that during class, spotting is key to safety! Spot every new skill, and stay with the student you are spotting until he or she can safely attempt it without assistance.

Keep It Moving

This idea explains itself. You lose students' attention, lose control of the class, and you may lose a student if a class is boring. Do not spend too much time on any one activity. Have music prepared in a playlist in advance so you do not have to change a CD or search for a song you want to use. Have mats and any props ready before class as well. Be ready to change directions and move on when the students become bored or start losing focus.

Repetition can be Different

Gymnastics skills are learned through repetition, which can become very boring to small (and sometimes older) students. You may hear parents say things like, "Susie's class is too easy. I want her moved up to the next level," or, "Anna has already learned how to do gymnastics, so we are going to try soccer." This is all because of the repetition needed to learn the skills. Students and parents do not understand that you always need the basics and will be improving on them throughout your entire gymnastics career. Adding different qualities and visual references to movement can enhance learning. Change starting positions and the pace of the movement. Change a station or drill so that it works across a mat. Change the parts of the skill on which to focus. Even when using the same lesson plan for a month, you can (and need to) make changes.

Theme It Up!

Themes can make any class more fun and vary the repetition. Pick a theme for each month of class. February could be hearts for Valentine's Day, May--flowers for springtime, and snowmen in December. Have small stuffed toys and cutouts for each theme, and incorporate them into the lesson plans. You will repeatedly find that the lesson plans call for a stuffed animal to hold onto or jump over; this is when you get to Theme It Up!

Gymnastics Class = Fun

Young students are in classes for fun and for love of movement. Parents want their children to enjoy the class over anything else. The hard work and training can come in later years. You need to be the best, coolest, most amazing focal point in the room. You need to hold students' attention by being FUN. Remember--we do not want students to get bored or distracted by things going on outside of their class. Do not be afraid to be silly, goofy, or funny. Keep your energy up! Always remind yourself that in order to keep you classes full, you need to make them fun!

If There Isn't a Choice, Don't Ask a Question

If you ask, "Don't you want to tumble?" you better be ready for the kid to say no. Never ask a question when you do not really want an answer. It is better to say, "Come and tumble." Also, do not make promises you cannot keep, such as, "We will play with the scarves next week." The students will remember you said this even if you do not. If you do not have a plan to do it or if you are not going to remember it, then do not say it. Asking for a line leader or someone to go first is always a problem in class as well. It can cause arguments and disappointment. Many teachers have different opinions on how to handle this. No one-way is right or wrong, but make your rule, explain your rule, and stick with it all year.

Praise the Good

We want students to model good behavior. This involves the good behavior of other students and of you! Bad behavior is what most students will tend to model, especially if bad behavior is what is getting your attention. Point out who is doing it right so other students will follow along. "Grace is pointing her toes, Anna is pointing her toes, Suzie is pointing her toes…" until you get everyone pointing their toes.

Be specific as to what good behavior is being exhibited; say the student's name and the specific thing he/she is doing well. "Good job" is not specific. You also want to limit negative attention. If students only hear their names when doing wrong, they are likely to quit listening. Another trick is to praise what you would like to be seeing. If students are not keeping their hands to themselves, do not jump right to, "Everyone needs to keep their hands to themselves." Instead say, "I love how everyone is keeping their hands to themselves." This will work with all kinds of behaviors—try it!

Conditioning is Important, Not a Punishment

Any athlete needs to be strong and gymnastics is no different. Although you do not need to be training mini body builders at a young age, you do want them to enjoy conditioning for proper muscle tone. Most kids grow to hate conditioning--they do not know why, but in modeling the behavior of adults, they learn to hate it. Make conditioning fun! Do it with your students, teach them the right way, and remember that no matter how much you might not want to do it with them, you do not want to be the one who teaches them to hate it.

Build Relationships

To keep students in your classes, first they need to have fun, and then they need to build relationships. If they have friends in class, they will be more likely to come back. The situation is similar with parents; when they stay in the building and talk (preferably a waiting room—not in the classroom area), they will make friendships with other parents and want all of their kids to continue taking the class together. Your relationship to students and their parents is equally important. Create "share time" with the class. If a student tells you he or she is doing something exciting the following week, remember it, and ask the student about it the next time you see him or her. Again, the same goes for parents; take notice of significant events in their lives and ask, compliment, or congratulate as appropriate.

Chapter Two
Introduction to Lesson Plans and Syllabi

There are three levels of lessons plans and syllabi labeled as Level 1, Level 2, and Level 3. These classes are all designed for younger students and work well with any combination of students, ages 2 – 7 years old. The syllabi for each level are the end result of that year's training; this is what the gymnast should be able to accomplish by the end of the year. There are gymnastics skills listed along with points of focus under each skill. You should not expect a perfect execution of the skills, but for the students to have mastered the major concepts listed with each skill. Since there are many different names for the same skill, I tried to explain the activity in clear terms. There are also additional concepts to consider in italics. These are progressions for the student who may master the skill faster than others. The goal is to keep them from getting bored.

Next there are ten months' worth of lesson plans for each level. For each month in all three levels, in addition to the skills, you will see share time, walking into the classroom, free movement, games, conditioning and story time. These are key components of creating structure in your classroom, building relationships with your students, and adding in a little extra fun.

When starting a class, it is important for students to line up in the entry area and walk in together. This keeps the students out of the classroom area so that you can finish your last class and/or prepare for the next class. It is also for safety reasons; keeping students off of the equipment when you are not supervising them prevents the potential for injury. It gives an official starting procedure to the class and helps the students understand that although gymnastics is fun, it is not free playtime.

Before walking into the classroom, I always stand with the students for about a minute at the entryway to the classroom area. This is used as our share time. I may ask them specific questions, but usually they already have something to tell me as soon as I get there.

Progressions are different skills students should do multiply times in a row down a long mat. This is a good time to stress good body positions and correct technique. The different stations are to be set up and done in a circuit with each student spending a minute or two at each station.

The skills contained within each lesson plan build on skills learned in previous lessons (where applicable). As the students progress, remember to use each skill in combination with other skills. For example, the lesson plan might say to do crab walks, forward rolls, and cartwheels during progressions. If your students have accomplished these skills, have them try to do all three in combination with one another, so that you are constantly keeping the students engaged.

The free movement sections involve a variety of props, improvisation, and music. This is usually students' favorite part of the class, since they get to move around freely and exercise their individual creativity; however, do not let this turn into students running around in circles for 3 minutes. Guide them by giving visuals and different types of music encouraging them to move in various ways. The games and directional songs are explained in Chapter 9.

The conditioning is short and sweet. This is included mainly for students to understand early on that conditioning is a part of gymnastics. Remember to make it fun, and be a good example by doing it with them.

The story time at the end of each class does not have to be anything specific. There are hundreds of childrens' books about taking gymnastics. All your students' favorite characters have had an adventure doing gymnastics at one point or another. The stories do not necessarily have to be about gymnastics, though. You can pick books based on your monthly theme or on an upcoming holiday. Only spend about 3 – 5 minutes reading at the end of the class. And remember, you do not have to finish a book each week--saving it to finish the following week will give students yet another reason to come back!

Always familiarize yourself with the lesson plan before the start of each class. Have all of your supplies out where you can access them easily during the transitions, and have your music on a playlist. This does not mean you will not have to think on your feet and make adjustments throughout the class depending on what is or is not working for your students on that particular day; however, being prepared makes the class run more smoothly when you do end up having to make changes.

Chapter Three

Level 1 Syllabus

Classroom Management

- Students sits with legs crossed and back to wall when asked
- Students understands taking turns
- Students walk to and from mat; does not, crawl, run, hop, etc.
- Students return to correct spot in line;

Floor

Army Drags

- Lay on stomach
- Uses arms and legs to crawl across the mat
- Does not go up on knees

Camel Walks

- Walks on hands and feet
- Keeps knees and elbows straight when walking

Chasé

- Dominate foot stays in front
- Feet meet in the air
- Arms side

Crab/Table Walks

- Walks on hands and feet with stomach towards the ceiling
- Travels full length of mat
- Crab walk bottom does not touch the ground
- *Walks forwards and backwards*
- *Table walk – stomach pushed up to ceiling*

Forward Rolls

- Start in bug with head down (chin on chest) at top of wedge mat
- Rolls straight, keeps head tucked
- *Rolls back onto feet*
- Stands up; *with out hands*
- *On floor without a wedge mat*

Frog Jumps

- Starts with hands and feet on ground
- Jumps high with arms up and body straight
- *Legs straight and together in the air*
- Lands with hands and feet on the ground

Hops Forward and Backwards

- Keeps foot up for full length of mat
- *Hops on 1 foot*

Jelly/Pencil Rolls

- Lays across mat on back
- Rolls straight down mat
- Jelly rolls; arms are by side
- *Pencil rolls; arms above head, hands together, elbows straight*
- *Legs straight, toes pointed*

Leap

- Transfers weight from 1 foot to the other
- Travels
- *Legs straight*
- *Toes pointed*

Lever

- Starts in a lunge
- Hits a T position with body
- Balances on 1 foot
- Arms by ears
- *Back leg straight*

Lunge

- Feet apart
- Front knee bent
- Back leg straight
- Arms up
- *Hips square*

Mini Cartwheel

- Starts with arms up
- Places hands on ground to the side
- Jumps feet over to other side of hands
- *Takes off and lands feet separately*

Mini Handstand

- Hands on ground with fingers forward
- Arms straight
- Head off ground
- Both feet leave the ground
- Can support body weight
- *Legs touch in the air*

Monkey Jumps

- Places both hand on the beam (or a raised mat)
- Jumps feet from one side of beam to the other
- Supports movement with straight arms
- *Lands on feet*

Seal Walks

- Stomach on the ground
- Lifts chest up supported by arms
- Uses arms to walk down the mat

Straddle Rolls

- Sits in a straddle position at top of a wedge mat
- Tucks head in; forward roll leaving legs in the straddle position
- *End in a straddle*

Wall Walkers (Stand wedge mat up against a wall)

- Arms straight
- Head off ground
- Both feet walk up the mat
- Can support body weight
- *Hits a handstand position*

Wall walkers with forward roll

- Hands on ground with fingers forward
- Arms straight
- Head off ground
- Both feet walk up the mat
- Can support body weight
- *Hits a handstand position*
- Tucks Head
- Rolls

Balance Beam

Balances in Arabesque

- Legs straight
- Toes pointed
- Keeps chest up
- Balances on 1 foot
- Arms out to side
- *Balances without assistance*

Balances in Passé

- Knee straight forward
- Side of foot touches at the knee of the supporting leg
- Arms out to side
- *Balances without assistance*

Bunny Hops

- Hops with feet together
- *Keeps toes forward on beam*

Kicks Forwards and Backwards

- Legs straight
- Toes pointed
- Keeps chest up
- Arms out to side
- *Travels without assistance*

V-sit

- Balances on bottom
- Legs Straight
- Body forms a V shape
- *Arms out to side*

Walks Forward and Backwards

- Keeps head up and arms straight out to sides
- Walks without assistance
- Places one foot in front of the other

Bars

Cast

- Arms Straight
- Swings legs together
- *Legs straight*
- *Toes pointed*
- *Lift hips off bar*

Front Support

- Supports body weight
- Does not lay stomach on the bar
- Arms straight
- *Legs straight*
- *Toes pointed*
- *Can jump up to a front support with out assistance*

Front Support Roll Down

- Holds onto bar
- Leans forward
- *Rolls down bringing feet to the ground*
- *Shows control*

Skin the cat

- Hangs from bar with both arms
- Brings both feet to bar
- Rotates through
- *Places feet on the ground*
- *Rotates back though to starting position*

Toes to the bar

- Hangs from bar with both arms
- Lifts toes to bar
- Legs straight
- *Holds position*

Vault/Mini Trampoline

Run, Jump, Stick with Springboard

- Hits springboard with 2 feet
- Allows board to push them into a jump
- Lands on feet
- *Sticks landing*

Straight Jumps on Springboard

- Arms up
- Jumps on springboard with 2 feet
- Jumps multiple times in a row
- Hits same spot on board
- *Allows board to push them into jumps*
- *Shows control*

Straight Jump onto Raised Mat

- Hits springboard with 2 feet
- Allows board to push them into a jump
- *Lands on feet*
- *Sticks landing*

Spilt Jumps

- 1 leg front and 1 leg back separating in the air
- Lands with feet together
- Arms side
- *Legs straight*
- *Toes pointed*

Straight Jump

- Arms up
- *Legs straight*
- *Toes pointed*

Straddle Jump

- Legs open in the air
- Lands with feet together
- *Knees pointed towards celling*

Tuck Jump

- Arms out to side
- Brings knees up towards chest
- *Does not kick their bottom*

Chapter Four

Level 1 Monthly Lesson Plans

Line up; Share time

Walk into room

Directional Songs

1. Hokey Pokey

2. Going on a Bear Hunt

Stretching – Together in a Circle

- Head – sideways, shoulder-to-shoulder, up and down, circle

- Arms – hug, arm circles, reaches right and left

- Touch toes

- Straddle – reach right, left and center

- Splits – right and left

Progressions

- Hops forward and backwards with two feet

- Pencil rolls

- Frog jumps

- Army drags

Free Movement – with Maracas

Stations

1. Wedge mat – Forward roll

2. Cartwheel mat – Monkey jumps

3. Beam – Walks forward

4. Trampoline – Tuck jumps

Conditioning – 5 of each

1. Sit-ups

2. Push-ups

3. Jumping jacks

Game – Parachute Games

Story

Line up; Share time

Walk into room

Directional Songs

1. Going on a Bear Hunt

2. Bean Bag Rock

Stretching – Dice Game

- Head – sideways, shoulder-to-shoulder, up and down, circle

- Arms – hug, arm circles, reaches right and left

- Touch toes

- Straddle – reach right, left and center

- Splits – right and left

Progressions

- Hops forward on one foot

- Crab walks

- Frog jumps

- Army drags

Free Movement – Scarves

Stations

1. Cartwheel mat – Monkey jumps
2. Wedge mat – Wall walkers
3. Bars – Toe touches
4. Hopscotch – (use chalk or tape to draw outline)

Conditioning – 5 of each

1. Push-ups
2. Jumping jacks
3. Lemon squeezers

Game – Musical Hula-hoops

Story

Line up; Share time

Walk into room

Directional Songs

1. Bean Bag Rock

2. Tony Chestnut

Stretching – Body Part Cards

- Head – sideways, shoulder-to-shoulder, up and down, circle

- Arms – hug, arm circles, reaches right and left

- Touch toes

- Straddle – reach right, left and center

- Splits – right and left

Progressions

- Table walks

- Seal walks

- Forward rolls

- Monkey jumps

Free Movement – with Ribbons

Stations

1. Wedge mat – Wall walkers
2. Cartwheel mat – Mini handstand
3. Beam – Kicks forward
4. Springboard – Straight jumps

Conditioning – 5 of each

1. Jumping jacks
2. Lemon squeezers
3. High knee runs

Game – Jump the Brook

Story

Line up; Share time

Walk into room

Directional Songs

1. Tony Chestnut

2. The Farmer in the Dell

Stretching – Deck of Cards Game

- Head – sideways, shoulder-to-shoulder, up and down, circle

- Arms – hug, arm circles, reaches right and left

- Touch toes

- Straddle – reach right, left and center

- Splits – right and left

Progressions

- Frog jumps

- Camel walks

- Forward rolls

- Monkey jumps

Free Movement – Animal Pictures

Stations

1. Cartwheel mat – Mini handstand

2. Wedge mat – Straddle rolls

3. Bars – Front support, cast

4. Trampoline – Straddle jumps

Conditioning – 5 of each

1. Lemon squeezers

2. High knee runs

3. Planks

Game – Toe Pick-up

Story

Line up; Share time

Walk into room

Directional Songs

1. The Farmer in the Dell

2. Bean Bag Catch

Stretching - Circuit

- Head – sideways, shoulder-to-shoulder, up and down, circle

- Arms – hug, arm circles, reaches right and left

- Touch toes

- Straddle – reach right, left and center

- Splits – right and left

Progressions

- Table walks

- Camel walks

- Hops backwards

- Monkey jumps

Free Movement – with Bubbles

Stations

1. Wedge mat – Straddle rolls

2. Cartwheel mat – Lunge, lever, lunge

3. Beam – V-sit

4. Hopscotch – with Hula-hoops

Conditioning – 5 of each

1. High knee runs

2. Planks

3. Leg raises

Game – Crab Ball

Story

Line up; Share time

Walk into room

Directional Songs

1. Bean Bag Catch

2. Bunny Hop

Stretching – Together in a Circle

- Head – sideways, shoulder-to-shoulder, up and down, circle

- Arms – hug, arm circles, reaches right and left

- Touch toes

- Straddle – reach right, left and center

- Splits – right and left

Progressions

- Seal walks

- Pencil rolls

- Frog jumps

- Straddle rolls

Free Movement – with Scarves

Stations

1. Cartwheel mat – Lunge, lever, lunge
2. Floor – Forward rolls, stand up
3. Bars – Hang and pick up objects with feet, place in bucket
4. Springboard – Run, straight jump, stick and finish

Conditioning – 5 of each

1. Planks
2. Leg raises
3. Burbees

Game – Parachute Games

Story

Line up; Share time

Walk into room

Directional Songs

1. Bunny Hop

2. Pass the Bean Bag

Stretching – Dice Game

- Head – sideways, shoulder-to-shoulder, up and down, circle

- Arms – hug, arm circles, reaches right and left

- Touch toes

- Straddle – reach right, left and center

- Splits – right and left

Progressions

- Army drags

- Chasé

- Table walks

- Straddle rolls

Free Movement – with Maracas

Stations

1. Floor – Forward roll, stand up

2. Cartwheel mat – Mini cartwheels

3. Beam – Bunny hops

4. Trampoline – Spilt jumps

Conditioning – 5 of each

1. Leg raises

2. Burbees

3. Lunges

Game – Musical Hula-hoops

Story

Line up; Share time

Walk into room

Directional Songs

1. Pass the Bean Bag

2. Head Shoulders Knees and Toes

Stretching – Body Part Cards

- Head – sideways, shoulder-to-shoulder, up and down, circle

- Arms – hug, arm circles, reaches right and left

- Touch toes

- Straddle – reach right, left and center

- Splits – right and left

Progressions

- Hop backwards

- Frog jump

- Camel walks

- Chasé

Free Movement – with Ribbons

Stations

1. Cartwheel mat – Mini cartwheels

2. Wedge mat – Wall walkers

3. Bars – Front support, roll down

4. Hopscotch – with place markers

Conditioning – 5 of each

1. Burbees

2. Lunges

3. Arm Circles

Game – Jump the Brook

Story

Line up; Share time

Walk into room

Directional Songs

1. Head Shoulders Knees and Toes

2. Animal Action

Stretching – Deck of Cards

- Head – sideways, shoulder-to-shoulder, up and down, circle

- Arms – hug, arm circles, reaches right and left

- Touch toes

- Straddle – reach right, left and center

- Splits – right and left

Progressions

- Table walks

- Forward rolls

- Mini cartwheels

- Seal walks

Free Movement – with Animal Pictures

Stations

1. Wedge mat – Wall walkers, forward roll

2. Cartwheel mat – Lunge, mini handstand, lunge

3. Beam – Passé walks

4. Springboard – Straight jump up onto raised mat

Conditioning – 5 of each

1. Lunges

2. Arm circles

3. Sit-ups

Game – Toe Pick-up

Story

Line up; Share time

Walk into room

Directional Songs

1. Animal Action

2. Hokey Pokey

Stretching – Circuit

- Head – sideways, shoulder-to-shoulder, up and down, circle

- Arms – hug, arm circles, reaches right and left

- Touch toes

- Straddle – reach right, left and center

- Splits – right and left

Progressions

- Forward rolls

- Mini cartwheels

- Hops forward and backwards

- Chasé leap

Free Movement – with Bubbles

Stations

1. Cartwheel mat – Lunge, mini handstand, lunge

2. Floor – Straddle roll

3. Bars – Skin the cat

4. Trampoline – Tuck jumps

Conditioning – 5 of each

1. Arm circles

2. Sit-ups

3. Push-ups

Game – Crab Ball

Story

Chapter Five
Level 2 Syllabus

Classroom Management

- Students sit with legs crossed and back to wall
- Students understand taking turns
- Walks to and from mat; does not, crawl, run, hop, etc.
- Returns to correct spot in line
- Students can complete all skills in level 1

Floor

Army Drags

- Lays on stomach
- Uses arms and legs to crawl across the mat
- Does not go up on knees

Backward Roll

- Starts in a squatting position with head down (chin on chest) at the top of wedge mat
- Rolls straight, keeps head tucked
- *Rolls back onto feet in squatting position*
- *Uses hands correctly*

Bridge

- Starts laying flat on back
- Pushes up using both hands and feet
- Stays off head
- *Fingers pointed toward feet*
- *Can push legs straight*
- *Keeps feet together*

Bridge Kick-over

- Completes all points under bridge
- Lift 1 leg up
- Kicks over
- *Shows split*
- *Legs straight*
- *Toes pointed*

Camel Walks

- Walks on hands and feet
- Keeps knees and elbows straight when walking

Candle Stick

- Lays on back with feet and legs pointed to celling
- Back off of ground
- Legs straight
- Toes pointed
- *Hands on ground not supporting body*

Crab/Table Walks

- Walks on hands and feet with stomach towards the ceiling
- Travels full length of mat
- Crab walk bottom does not touch the ground
- Walks forwards and backwards
- Table walk stomach pushed up to ceiling creating a table

Donkey Kicks

- Supports body weight with hands
- Kicks both feet up at same time

Forward Rolls

- Start in a squatting position with head down (chin on chest)
- Rolls straight, keeps head tucked
- Rolls back onto feet in squatting position without pushing with hands

Frog Jumps

- Starts with hands and feet ground
- Jumps high with arms up and body straight
- Legs straight and together in the air
- Lands with hands and feet ground

Handstand Forward Roll

- Kicks up to handstand with hands on ground against the top part of wedge mat
- Tucks head and rolls down wedge mat
- Stands up without using hands
- *Holds handstand position*
- *On floor without wedge mat*

Hops on one foot, forward/backwards

- Keeps foot up for full length of mat
- *Can do with either right or left foot up, not just on one side*

Pencil Rolls

- Lay across mat on back
- Rolls straight down mat
- Arms above head, hands together, elbows straight
- Legs straight, toes pointed

Lever

- Starts in a lunge
- Hits a T position with body
- Balances on 1 foot
- Arms by ears
- Back leg straight
- Toe pointed

Lunge

- Feet apart
- Front knee bent
- Back leg straight
- Hips square
- Arms up

Mini Cartwheel

- Starts with arms up
- Places hands on ground to the side
- Jumps feet over to other side of hands
- Takes off and lands feet separately

Mini Handstand

- Hands on ground with fingers forward
- Arms straight
- Head off ground
- Both feet leave the ground
- Can support body weight

Monkey Jumps

- Place both hand on a raised mat
- Jumps feet from one side of a mat to the other
- Supports movement with straight arms
- Lands on feet

Safety Roll

- Forward roll from standing position with out using hands
- Tucks head

Seal Walks

- Stomach on the ground
- Lifts chest up supported by arms
- Uses arms to walk down the mat

Skips

- Alternates feet

Straddle Forward Rolls

- Sits in a straddle position
- Tucks head in and do a forward roll leaving legs in the straddle position
- Ends in a straddle position

Wall Walkers with Forward Roll

- Hands on ground with fingers forward
- Arms straight
- Head off ground
- Both feet walk up the mat
- Can support body weight
- Hits a handstand position
- Tucks head
- Rolls

Balance Beam

Balances in Arabesque

- Leg straight
- Toes pointed
- Keeps chest up
- Balances on 1 foot.
- Arms out to side
- Balances without assistance

Balances in Passé

- Knee straight forward
- Side of foot touches at the knee of the supporting leg
- Arms out to side
- Balances without assistance

Bunny Hops

- Hops with feet together
- Keeps toes forward on beam

Kicks Forwards and Backwards

- Leg straight
- Toes pointed
- Keeps chest up
- Arms out to side
- Travels without assistance

V-sit

- Balances on bottom
- Legs straight
- Body forms a V shape
- Arms out to side

Walks Forward and Backwards

- Keeps head up and arms straight out to sides
- Walks without assistance
- Places one foot in front of the other

Bars

Cast

- Arms Straight
- Legs straight
- Toes pointed
- Swings legs together
- *Lift hips off bar*

Front Support

- Supports body weight
- Does not lay stomach on the bar
- Arms straight
- Legs straight
- Toes pointed
- *Can jump to front support with out assistance*

Front Support Roll Down

- Holds onto bar
- Leans forward
- Rolls down bringing feet to the ground
- *Shows control*

Skin the Cat

- Hangs from bar with both arms
- Brings both feet to bar
- Rotates through
- Places feet on the ground
- *Rotates back though to starting position*

Toes to the Bar

- Hangs from bar with both arms
- Lifts toes to bar
- Legs straight
- Holds position

Vault/Mini Trampoline

Run, Jump, Stick with Springboard

- Hits springboard with 2 feet
- Allows board to push them into a jump
- Lands on feet
- Sticks landing

Straight Jumps on Springboard

- Arms up
- Jumps on springboard with 2 feet
- Jumps multiple times in a row
- Hits same spot on board
- Allows board to push them into jumps
- *Shows control*

Straight Jump onto raised mat

- Jumps on springboard with 2 feet
- Allows board to push them into a jump
- Lands on feet
- Sticks landing

Squat On

- Jumps on springboard with 2 feet
- Places hands on raised mat before feet
- Lands on feet
- Lands on raised mat in a squat position
- *Feet and knees together*

Spilt Jumps

- 1 leg front and 1 leg back separating in the air
- Lands with feet together
- Arms side
- Legs straight
- Toes pointed

Straight Jump

- Arms up
- Legs straight
- Toes pointed

Straddle Jump

- Legs open in the air
- Lands with feet together
- *Knees pointed towards celling*

Tuck Jump

- Arms out to side
- Brings knees up towards chest
- Does not kick their bottom

Chapter Six

Level 2 Monthly Lesson Plans

Line up; Share time

Walk into room

Directional Songs

1. Bunny Hop

2. Bean Bag Rock

Stretching – Together in a Circle

- Head – sideways, shoulder-to-shoulder, up and down, circle

- Arms – hug, arm circles, reaches right and left

- Touch toes

- Straddle – reach right, left and center

- Splits – right, left and center

Progressions

- Seal walks

- Army drags

- Table walks

- Pencil rolls

Free Movement – with Ribbons

Stations

1. Wedge mat – Forward roll

2. Floor – Mini cartwheel

3. Bars – Front support, roll down

4. Table walks around cones

Conditioning – 10 of each

1. Sit-ups

2. Push-ups

3. Jumping jacks

Games

1. Parachute Games

2. Mother May I

Story

Line up; Share time

Walk into room

Directional Songs

1. Bean Bag Rock

2. Animal Actions

Stretching – Dice Game

- Head – sideways, shoulder-to-shoulder, up and down, circle

- Arms – hug, arm circles, reaches right and left

- Touch toes

- Straddle – reach right, left and center

- Splits – right, left and center

Progressions

- Army drags

- Table walks

- Pencil rolls

- Hops on one foot

Free Movement –with Animal Pictures

Stations

1. Floor – Mini cartwheel

2. Wedge mat – Wall walkers, forward roll

3. Beam – V-sit

4. Springboard – Run, jump, stick and finish

Conditioning – 10 of each

1. Push-ups

2. Jumping jacks

3. Lemon squeezers

Games

1. Mother May I

2. Musical Hula-hoops

Story

Line up; Share time

Walk into room

Directional Songs

1. Animal Actions

2. Pass the Bean Bag

Stretching – Body Part Game

- Head – sideways, shoulder-to-shoulder, up and down, circle

- Arms – hug, arm circles, reaches right and left

- Touch toes

- Straddle – reach right, left and center

- Splits – right and left

Progressions

- Safety rolls

- Camel walks

- Mini cartwheels

- Hops on one foot

Free Movement – with Bubbles

Stations

1. Wedge mat – Wall walkers, forward roll
2. Floor – Lunge, level, mini-handstand
3. Bars – Front support, 3 cast
4. Trampoline – Spilt jumps

Conditioning – 10 of each

1. Jumping jacks
2. Lemon squeezers
3. High knees

Games

1. Musical Hula-hoops
2. Red Light, Green Light

Story

Line up; Share time

Walk into room

Directional Songs

1. Pass the Bean Bag

2. The Farmer in the Dell

Stretching – Card Game

- Head – sideways, shoulder-to-shoulder, up and down, circle

- Arms – hug, arm circles, reaches right and left

- Touch toes

- Straddle – reach right, left and center

- Splits – right, left and center

Progressions

- Table walks

- Pencil rolls

- Hops on one foot

- Hops on one foot backwards

Free Movement – with Scarves

Stations

1. Floor – Lunge, level, mini-handstand

2. Wedge mat – Backward roll

3. Beam – Kicks front and back

4. Hopscotch – Draw lines with chalk or tape

Conditioning – 10 of each

1. Lemon squeezers

2. High knees

3. Planks

Games

1. Read Light, Green Light

2. Jump the Brook

Story

Line up; Share time

Walk into room

Directional Songs

1. The Farmer in the Dell

2. Bean Bag Catch

Stretching - Circuit

- Head – sideways, shoulder-to-shoulder, up and down, circle

- Arms – hug, arm circles, reaches right and left

- Touch toes

- Straddle – reach right, left and center

- Splits – right, left and center

Progressions

- Pencil rolls

- Hops on one foot

- Hops on one foot backwards

- Forward rolls

Free Movement – with Maracas

Stations

1. Wedge mat – Backward roll

2. Floor - Cartwheel

3. Bars – Skin the cat

4. Springboard – Run, jump, land on raised mat

Conditioning – 10 of each

1. High knees

2. Planks

3. Leg raises

Games

1. Jump the Brook

2. "Miss Gina" Says

Story

Line up; Share time

Walk into room

Directional Songs

    1. Bean Bag Catch

    2. Tony Chest Nut

Stretching – Together in a Circle

- Head – sideways, shoulder-to-shoulder, up and down, circle

- Arms – hug, arm circles, reaches right and left

- Touch toes

- Straddle – reach right, left and center

- Splits – right, left and center

Progressions

- Table walks

- Camel walks

- Forward rolls

- Mini cartwheels

Free Movement – with Ribbons

Stations

1. Floor - Cartwheel

2. Wedge mat - Bridge

3. Beam – Hops over stuffed animals

4. Tramp – Review jumps

Conditioning – 10 of each

1. Planks

2. Leg raises

3. Burbees

Games

1. "Miss Gina" Says

2. Toe Pick-up

Story

Line up; Share time

Walk into room

Directional Songs

1. Tony Chestnut

2. Head, Shoulders, Knees and Toes

Stretching – Dice Game

- Head – sideways, shoulder-to-shoulder, up and down, circle

- Arms – hug, arm circles, reaches right and left

- Touch toes

- Straddle – reach right, left and center

- Splits – right, left and center

Progressions

- Camel walks

- Forward rolls

- Mini cartwheels

- Step, hop - skips

Free Movement – with Animal Pictures

Stations

1. Floor – Bridge
2. Wedge Mat – Handstand, forward roll
3. Bars – Pick up stuffed animals with feet and put in a bucket
4. Candle stick, stand up

Conditioning – 10 of each

1. Leg raises
2. Burbees
3. Lunges

Games

1. Toe – Pick Up
2. Kangaroo Hop

Story

Line up; Share time

Walk into room

Directional Songs

1. Head Shoulders, Knees and Toes

2. Hokey Pokey

Stretching – Body Part Game

- Head – sideways, shoulder-to-shoulder, up and down, circle

- Arms – hug, arm circles, reaches right and left

- Touch toes

- Straddle – reach right, left and center

- Splits – right, left and center

Progressions

- Safety rolls

- Mini cartwheels

- Step, hop – skips

- Frog jumps

Free Movement – with Bubbles

Stations

1. Wedge Mat – Handstand, forward roll

2. Floor – Backward roll

3. Beam – V-sit, stand up

4. Springboard – Squat on

Conditioning – 10 of each

1. Burbees

2. Lunges

3. Arm circles

Games

1. Kangaroo Hop

2. Crab Ball

Story

Line up; Share time

Walk into room

Directional Songs

1. Hokey Pokey

2. Going on a Bear Hunt

Stretching – Card Game

- Head – sideways, shoulder-to-shoulder, up and down, circle

- Arms – hug, arm circles, reaches right and left

- Touch toes

- Straddle – reach right, left and center

- Splits – right, left and center

Progressions

- Safety roll

- Donkey kicks

- Step, hop – skips

- Seal walks

Free Movement – with Scarves

Stations

1. Floor – Backward roll

2. Floor – Run, cartwheel

3. Bars – Front Support, ½ roll down and back up

4. Hopscotch – with Hula-hoops

Conditioning – 10 of each

1. Lunges

2. Arm circles

3. Sit-ups

Games

1. Crab Ball

2. Balloon Toss

Story

Line up; Share time

Walk into room

Directional Songs

1. Going on a Bear Hunt

2. Bunny Hop

Stretching - Circuit

- Head – sideways, shoulder-to-shoulder, up and down, circle

- Arms – hug, arm circles, reaches right and left

- Touch toes

- Straddle – reach right, left and center

- Splits – right and left

Progressions

- Donkey kicks

- Backward rolls

- Frog jumps

- Table walks – balance stuffed animal on stomach

Free Movement – with Maracas

Stations

1. Floor – Run, cartwheel

2. Wedge mat – Bridge kick-over

3. Beam – Walks; front, side and backwards

4. Springboard – Run, squat on, jump off, stick, finish

Conditioning – 10 of each

1. Arm circles

2. Sit-ups

3. Push-ups

Games

1. Balloon Toss

2. Parachute Games

Story

Chapter Seven

Level 3 Syllabus

Classroom Management Points

- Students are able to complete all skills in Level 1 and Level 2
- Students stand in a line and waits for turn during progressions
- Students remember each station rotation

Floor

Back Bend

- Completes back bend on a wedge mat
- *Complete Back Bend on the floor*
- *Able to land without head touching the ground*

Backward Straddle Roll

- Starts standing in a straddle position
- Backward roll leaving legs in the straddle position
- End standing in a straddle position

Bridge Kick-over

- Completes all points under bridge
- Lift 1 leg up
- Kicks over
- Shows split
- Legs straight
- Toes pointed

Cartwheel

- Starts with arms up, in a lunge
- Places hands on ground to the side
- Jumps feet over to other side of hands
- Takes off and lands feet separately
- *Hits a vertical position with legs in a straddle*

Handstand

- Starts in lunge
- Supports body weight
- Keeps arms straight, head does not touch ground
- Feet touch in air

Handstand to Bridge

- All points in handstand
- Feet come down together into a bridge
- *Shows control*

Handstand Forward Roll

- Kicks up to handstand with hands on ground against the top part of wedge mat
- Tucks head and rolls down wedge mat
- Stands up without using hands
- Holds handstand position
- *On floor without wedge mat*

Leap

- Transfers weight from 1 foot to the other
- Travels
- Legs straight
- Toes pointed

Round-off

- Supports body weight
- Lands with 2 feet
- *Feet meet in the air*

Table Walks

- Travels full length of mat

- Walks forwards and backwards

- Stomach pushed up to ceiling creating a table

Beam

½ Turn

- Starts in passé

- Completes ½ of turn

- Steps forward to finish

1 Leg Hops

- Holds beam with both hands

- Balances with one foot in the air

- Hops down beam

- Supports weight with arms

Cartwheel off end of Beam

- Starts in a lunge

- Hands on beam, all 10 fingers on the same side of beam

- Supports body weight

- Both feet leave the beam

- *Both feet land separately on the floor off the end of the beam*

Knee Scale

- Kneels on beam
- One leg stretched out straight
- Both hands on the beam
- Supports body weight
- *Shows control*

Leap

- Transfers weight from 1 foot to the other
- Travels
- Legs straight
- Toes pointed

Lever

- Leaves from a lunge
- Hits a T position with body
- Balances on 1 foot
- Arms by ears
- Back leg straight
- Toe pointed

V-sit Stand up

- Balances on bottom
- Legs straight
- Body forms a V shape
- Arms out to side
- Stands up
- *Stands up with out using hands*
- *Show control*

Bars

Basket Swing

- All points from leg cut
- Swings backward
- Hooks knee around bar
- *Swings back up to starting position*

Cast

- Arms straight
- Legs straight
- Toes pointed
- Swings legs together
- Lift hips off bar

Leg Cuts

- Starts in a front support
- Brings dominate leg over the top of the bar
- Places one hand on either side of leg
- *Supports body weight with arms and does not sit on the bar*

Pull Over

- Kicks both feet over the bar
- Circles body around bar
- Lifts chest up to front support
- *Lifts both legs at the same time*
- *Legs straight*
- *Toes pointed*

Straddle Hang

- Hangs from bar with both arms
- Lifts toes to bar in a straddle
- Legs straight
- *Holds position*

Vault

Arm Circle

- Reaches both arms forward
- Arms make a complete circle
- *Arms end up by ears in a tight finish position*

Handstand Fall Flat

- Starts in a lunge
- Hits handstand position
- Falls flat onto back
- Body stays tight
- *Lands in a tight body position, does not roll body down*

Straddle On

- Jumps on springboard with 2 feet
- Places hands on raised mat before feet
- Lands on feet
- Lands on raised mat in a straddle position
- Legs straight

Squat On

- Jumps on springboard with 2 feet
- Places hands on raised mat before feet
- Lands on feet
- Lands on raised mat in a squat position
- Feet and knees together

Chapter Eight

Level 3 Monthly Lesson Plans

Line up; Share time

Walk into room

Directional Songs

1. The Farmer in the Dell

2. Bean Bag Catch

Stretching – Together in a circle

- Arms and wrist

- Straddle and pike stretch

- Splits – right, left and center

- Bridge

Progressions

- Frog jumps

- Army drags

- Pencil rolls

- Table walks

Free Movement – with Bubbles

Stations

1. Floor – Run, cartwheel

2. Wedge mat – Bridge kick-over

3. Beam – Kicks

4. Bars – Straddle hang

5. Springboard – Squat on

Conditioning – 15 of each

1. Sit-ups

2. Push-ups

3. Jumping jacks

Games

1. Balloon Toss

2. Kangaroo Hop

Story

Line up; Share time

Walk into room

Directional Songs

1. Bean Bag Catch

2. Tony Chestnut

Stretching – Dice Game

- Arms and wrist

- Straddle and pike stretch

- Splits – right, left and center

- Bridge

Progressions

- Army drags

- Pencil rolls

- Camel walks

- Skips

Free Movement – with Animal Pictures

Stations

1. Wedge mat – Bridge kick-over

2. Floor – Forward roll

3. Beam – Leaps over stuffed animal

4. Bars – Big cast

5. Trampoline – Straddle jumps

Conditioning – 15 of each

1. Push-ups

2. Jumping jacks

3. Lemon squeezers

Games

1. Kangaroo Hop

2. "Miss Gina" Says

Story

Line up; Share time

Walk into room

Directional Songs

1. Tony Chestnut

2. Pass the Bean Bag

Stretching – Body Part Game

- Arms and wrist

- Straddle and pike stretch

- Splits – right, left and center

- Bridge

Progressions

- Camel walks

- Seal walks

- Hop forward

- Hop backward

Free Movement – with ribbons

Stations

1. Floor – Forward roll

2. Wedge mat – Handstand forward roll

3. Beam – Lung, lever, lunge

4. Bars – Leg cuts

5. Springboard – Straddle on

Conditioning – 15 of each

1. Jumping jacks

2. Lemon squeezers

3. High knees

Games

1. "Miss Gina" Says

2. Red Light, Green Light

Story

Line up; Share time

Walk into room

Directional Songs

1. Pass the Bean Bag

2. Head Shoulders Knees and Toes

Stretching – Card Game

- Arms and wrist

- Straddle and pike stretch

- Splits – right, left and center

- Bridge

Progressions

- Hops forward on 1 foot

- Hops backward one 1 foot

- Forward rolls

- Chasé

Free Movement – with Maracas

Stations

1. Wedge Mat – Handstand, forward roll

2. Floor – Round-off

3. Beam – 1 Leg hops

4. Bars – Pull-over

5. Trampoline – Tuck jumps

Conditioning – 15 of each

1. Lemon squeezers

2. High knees

3. Planks

Games

1. Red Light, Green Light

2. Mother May I

Story

Line up; Share time

Walk into room

Directional Songs

1. Head Shoulders Knees and Toes

2. Animal Action

Stretching – Circuit

- Arms and wrist

- Straddle and pike stretch

- Splits – right, left and center

- Bridge

Progressions

- Forward rolls

- Chasé, leap

- Table walks

- Cartwheels

Free Movement – with Scarves

Stations

1. Floor – Round-off

2. Wedge Mat – Backward roll

3. Beam – Cartwheel off end

4. Bars – Basket swing

5. Springboard – Run, jump, stick

Conditioning – 15 of each

1. High knees

2. Planks

3. Leg raises

Games

1. Mother May I

2. Crab Ball

Story

Line up; Share time

Walk into room

Directional Songs

1. Animal Action

2. Bean Bag Rock

Stretching – Together in a Circle

- Arms and wrist

- Straddle and pike stretch

- Splits – Right, left and center

- Bridge

Progressions

- Cartwheel

- Forward straddle roll

- Frog jump

- Army drag

Free Movement – with Bubbles

Stations

1. Floor – Backward roll

2. Wedge mat - Handstand

3. Beam – Arabesque

4. Bars – Hang and pick things up with feet

5. Trampoline – Pike jumps

Conditioning – 15 of each

1. Planks

2. Leg raises

3. Burbees

Games

1. Crab Ball

2. Toe Pick Up

Story

Line up; Share time

Walk into room

Directional Songs

1. Bean Bag Rock

2. Hokey Pokey

Stretching – Dice Game

- Arms and wrist

- Straddle and pike stretch

- Splits – right, left and center

- Bridge

Progressions

- Backward rolls

- Seal walks

- Frog jumps

- Camel walks

Free Movement – with Animal Pictures

Stations

1. Wedge mat – Handstand

2. Floor – Straddle roll

3. Beam – Knee scale

4. Bars – Straddle hang

5. Springboard – Run, hurdle, jump with arm circle

Conditioning – 15 of each

1. Leg raises

2. Burbees

3. Lunges

Games

1. Toe Pick Up

2. Jump the Brook

Story

Line up; Share time

Walk into room

Directional Songs

1. Hokey Pokey

2. Bunny Hop

Stretching – Body Part Game

- Arms and wrist

- Straddle and pike stretch

- Splits – right, left and center

- Bridge

Progressions

- Backward straddle rolls

- Pencil rolls

- Hops backward on 1 foot

- Skips

Free Movement – with Ribbons

Stations

1. Floor – Straddle roll

2. Wedge mat - Backbend

3. Beam – V-sit, stand up

4. Bars – Big cast

5. Trampoline – Split jumps

Conditioning – 15 of each

1. Burbees

2. Lunges

3. Arm circles

Games

1. Jump the Brook

2. Musical Hula-hoops

Story

Line up; Share time

Walk into room

Directional Songs

1. Bunny Hop

2. Going on a Bear Hunt

Stretching – Cards Game

- Arms and wrist

- Straddle and pike stretch

- Splits – right, left and center

- Bridge

Progressions

- Table walks

- Cartwheels

- Chasé, leap

- Frog jumps

Free Movement – with Maracas

Stations

1. Wedge mat – Backbend

2. Floor – Handstand to a bridge

3. Beam – ½ turn

4. Bars – Leg cut, basket swing

5. Springboard – Run straight Jump, handstand fall flat

Conditioning – 15 of each

1. Lunges

2. Arm circles

3. Sit-ups

Games

1. Musical Hula-hoops

2. Parachute Games

Story

Line up; Share time

Walk into room

Directional Songs

1. Going on a Bear Hunt

2. The Farmer in the Dell

Stretching - Circuit

- Arms and wrist

- Straddle and pike stretch

- Splits – right, left and center

- Bridge

Progressions

- Forward rolls

- Backward rolls

- Forward straddle rolls

- Cartwheels

Free Movement – with Scarves

Stations

    1. Floor – Handstand to a bridge

    2. Floor – Run, round-off

    3. Beam – Leap

    4. Bars – Pull over, cast

    5. Trampoline – any jump

Conditioning – 15 of each

    1. Arm circles

    2. Sit-ups

    3. Push-ups

Games

    1. Parachute

    2. Balloon Toss

Story

Chapter Nine
Games, Directional Songs, and Supplies

Directional Songs

The following directional songs can be found on many different Children's CD's, by various artists. The song tells the various motions to do while you listen and follow along with your students.

"The Hokey Pokey"

"Head, Shoulders, Knees and Toes"

"I'm Going on a Bear Hunt"

"Tony Chestnut"

"The Farmer in the Dell"

"Animal Action"

"Bean Bag Catch"

"Bean Bag Rock"

"Bunny Hop"

Games

Balloon Toss

Using 3 - 5 balloons have the students try to keep all the balloons in the air any way they can without holding on to them. As the game progresses have them try it with out using their hands.

Crab Ball

In a crab walk position; kick a balloon back and forth. As the game progresses try not letting the balloon touch the ground.

"If You're Happy and You Know It" with Parachute

Sing the directional song, "If You're Happy and You Know It," but add in directions you can do with the parachute, such as: up and down, side-to-side, shake, etc.

Jump the Brook

Place two jump ropes parallel on the ground. Let your students try to "jump over the brook." Move the ropes farther a part after each student jumps.

Kangaroo Hop

Students start at one side of the room. Have them place a beanbag or stuffed animal between their knees. Students try to jump all the way across the room.

"Miss Gina" Says

This is played just like the game Simon Says, but you use your own name instead. Remember to use gymnastics terms, because this is a great game for testing students to see if they know the names of different gymnastics skills.

Mother, May I?

The leader gives directions to the group or an individual student. The student or group must ask, "Mother, may I?" before moving. The leader then replies, "Yes, you may," before the student can complete the direction. If a student does not ask, "Mother may I," and/or if the leader says, "No, you may not," the players stay where they are. Vary the game by adding different tumbling movements; for example, the directions could be to do 2 monkey jumps, or 3 rolls.

Musical Hula-hoops

Make a path of hula-hoops and have the students travel from hoop to hoop as the music plays. When the music stops, each student freezes inside one hoop. As the game progresses, remove one hoop at a time. Either eliminate students not in a hoop until one is left, as in Musical Chairs, or have the students share their hoop with another student. Reduce the hoops until all students are sharing one or two hoops when the music stops.

Parachute Tag

Lift the parachute high overhead. Call one student's name and have him or her run (or skip, hop, twirl, crawl, etc.) to the other side before the parachute comes down and tags them.

Parachute with Beanbags

Throw a few beanbags on top of the parachute, and see if you can get them to stay on while moving the parachute. Next, try to get them off as fast as you can.

Red Light, Green Light

Have the students line up at one end of the room. The leader stands at the other end of the room and turns their back to the other Students. When the leader says, "green light," the students walk toward the leader. When the leader says, "red light," the students must stop. As soon as the leader says red light, he/she turns around to catch any student still moving. Any students caught still walking are sent back to the starting line. If the students are very young, just call out the names of the ones still moving and try again.

Toe Pick Up

In a crab walk position, pick up small objects with your toes and put them in a bucket, as the game progress have them try picking up all of the yellow objects, then the blue, then red, etc.

Free Movement

The free movement involves a variety of props, improvisation, and music. Guide them by giving visuals as well as different types of music, and then have them move as to how it makes them feel. For the free movement with animal pictures, find 5 pictures of different animals. Show a picture and then have the students move to the music as if they were the animals. The free movement is students' favorite part of class, since they get to move around freely and exercise their individual creativity. Remember do not let this turn into students running around in circles for 3 minutes.

Stretching

Body Part Game

Print out pictures, or write on cards, different parts of the body. For example, head, arms, feet, legs etc. Have each student draw a card and then pick a stretch that fits the body part they drew.

Card Game

Have 10 – 15 playing cards (numbers only). Have a student call out a stretch and then draw a card. Have the students hold the stretch counting to the number on the card.

Circuit

Designate areas of the gym for each stretch by writing on cards or printing out pictures. Have students start at different stations. Have them complete the stretch for a minute and then have them run to the next station. Do this until each student has completed each stretch in the circuit.

Dice Game

Using a large dice, have each student roll the dice. Then hold the stretch counting to the number that the student rolled.

Supplies and Equipment

- Animal pictures
- Balloon
- Bar
- Beam
- Bean bags
- Body part cards
- Bubbles
- Bucket
- Cartwheel mat
- Circuit cards
- Cones
- Deck of cards
- Dice
- Hula-hoops
- Maracas
- Panel mats
- Parachute
- Place holders
- Ribbons
- Scarves

- Softer mat

- Spotting block

- Springboard

- Stuffed animals and shapes

- Trampoline

- Wedge mat

Made in the USA
Middletown, DE
01 March 2018